CODING FOR ABSOLUTE BEGINNERS

How to Keep Your Data Safe from Hackers by Mastering the Basic Functions of Python, Java, and C++ (2022 Guide for Newbies)

Eric Vargas

TABLE OF CONTENTS

INTRODUCTION

So you want to learn to code but don't know where to begin? This book will be your one-stop-shop for all things coding. We'll give you a quick overview of what coding is and how it can help you in any industry, and then we'll explain why it's important for everyone from high school students to seniors. We will also provide some resources for free learning and teaching yourself more advanced skills on your own time.

What exactly is coding?

Coding is the process of converting instructions into a computer language. This code can be understood by the computer, and the code can control how the computer functions, allowing people to achieve their goals. Coding is one of America's fastest-growing and highest-paying jobs. (2015) (Bureau of Labor Statistics) If you've ever used an ATM or a credit card to pay for something, coding was probably involved.

How does it function?

A programmer writes code with the help of special programs on your computer keyboard or a text editor, such as Notepad on Windows or TextEdit on OS X. The code, like the instructions on a piece of paper, tells the computer what to do or how to function. This code can assist a person in doing anything that requires programming skills, such as creating games, connecting electronic devices, programming robots, and much more.

What is the significance of this?

Every industry requires programming skills. Many jobs in technology, such as software engineers, technicians, and IT specialists, require coding. Other positions in technology, in addition to these, do not require programming skills at all, but rather an expertise in specific programs and languages. Coding is frequently used in schools to teach students all of the skills required for academic success a wide range of industries Coding can provide students with the experience they need to make something happen, learn to be self-sufficient and creative, and work well under pressure. There's nothing to be concerned about; it's just programming!

Where can I find out more?

There are numerous resources available on the internet to help you get started. Many resources, such as Codecademy, Code Academy, Lynda.com, and Udemy, are available online for free or for a small fee. You might even want to try your hand at writing code from scratch if you have any ideas. All you need is a computer, an internet connection, and a little drive.

Goals should be coded!

This is just the tip of the iceberg in terms of where coding can take you in your life! You will be able to use this knowledge to learn more advanced skills that will be more meaningful to you on your own time, such as teaching yourself how to use advanced software languages such as C++ or Python. Perhaps you'll become a web designer and build your websites or applications to help you learn more about your abilities. Take advantage of this once-in-a-lifetime opportunity!

Coding is just one step in the larger technology industry, and anyone can take it with you. It's as much fun as it sounds and will teach you skills that you can use throughout your life. We'll see you there if you're ready to dive in!

CHAPTER 1:

DEFINITIONS OF COMMON TERMS

Coding is the process of converting a problem into code or a string of symbols and language that a computer can understand.

HTML: Hypertext markup language, or how your website's information is presented to users. HTML is a markup language that is used to format text, images, links, video, and audio.

JavaScript: A web development programming language that makes it easier to create interactive websites and add effects such as scrolling boxes and drop-down menus. JavaScript enables you to create more dynamic pages that perform faster than static pages produced from pure HTML.

Node.js is a JavaScript framework that enables you to create powerful real-time applications by utilizing an event-driven and non-blocking I/O model.

jQuery: A JavaScript library for rapid web development that simplifies HTML document traversal, event handling, animation, and Ajax interactions.

Responsive Design: The process of adapting a website's design to different screen sizes (smartphones, tablets, laptops, etc.) without affecting the website's layout or functionality.

Test-Driven Development (TDD) is a method or framework for automating software testing that is based on creating test cases from an incomplete specification. It asserts that code should be specified before it is written.

Coding's fundamental terms.

1. Abbreviation: A text or a group of words that has been shortened.

The most common application is to give organizations a short and memorable name so that people can remember them easily. It is also used informally to express complex concepts or ideas by using only a portion of the entire world, which saves time when reading.The abbreviation, as well as typing it For example, "Max" in "Maxwell" can also be used to describe a variable in math formulas, and "X1000" may be used to describe a million (1000x) rather than an actual number (1x1000).

2. Accessibility: The ease with which content on a website or other media can be accessed. The accessibility of a website is comprised of many different factors, including design, content, and technology.

3.API-API stands for application programming interface. A collection of routines, protocols, and tools used to create software applications.

4. Cache: Temporary storage available on your computer's or mobile device's web browser that stores data faster or more efficiently than it is retrieved from the site itself. It enables the browser to load websites faster by storing frequently accessed web page elements such as text, graphics, and sounds. Caching also allows users to access online information even when no Internet connection is available.

5. Challenge-response authentication: A type of security protocol in which a user is first challenged to provide some information about themselves and then presented with a response based on that original information that they must enter or re-enter in order to proceed.

6. Character encoding: The process of converting textual data into a sequence of (usually) 8-bit characters using an alphabet and/or character set.

7. Command line: A command line is a text-based method of communicating with a computer's operating system, programs, and applications via typed commands. Instead of using the mouse or graphical interfaces, it is primarily used for programming or performing simple tasks such as compiling code or opening programs via the command line.

8. Configuration: The process of identifying and defining the settings with which a device communicates when it is in use.

9. CYA: (Also known as CAPS) Another acronym that meant all of the above was courtesy. It is frequently used in the design of user interfaces.

10. Contextual Accessibility: The ease with which a person can gain access to content on a website or other media in light of its current context (location, time, task). Contextual accessibility is about recognizing the context in which people are using technology at any given time while online and using it to meet their needs appropriately—according to their current needs and interests.

11. Digital Divide: The difference between individuals, households, and communities who have access to the internet and digital resources available online and those who do not.

12. Encoding: The process of converting information into strings of symbols that can be transmitted, stored, or processed by a computer. ASCII, which represents text as a sequence of numbers ranging from 0 to 255, is a common example of encoding

13. File Extension: The suffix that appears after the period/dot symbol at the end of a file name (ex: .html). It indicates the type of file, such as.html for HTML files.

14. Globalization: The process of adapting content (such as information and software) from one language and cultural context to another.

15. Hyperlink: A type of reference (a link) that connects two or more locations on the same website. A hyperlink usually opens a new window or tab in a web browser and reads the referenced text or image at that location.

16. Internet Explorer: A set of graphical user interface (GUI) web browsers created by Microsoft for Windows systems that support HTML 4 and CSS 2 selectors as well as ActiveX controls.

17. Internet search engine: A type of web search that searches the entire World Wide Web for documents that contain the relevant keywords and returns those that are most likely to contain this information rather than directly retrieving text data from a specific source.

18. JavaScript: A programming language created by Netscape that was first released in 1995. It is an object-oriented scripting language that can be embedded in client-side web pages or run as a standalone program to generate interactive experiences on the browser's client-side.

19. JavaScript: (JavaScript) is a programming language that allows developers to create dynamic web pages and applications that can be run within a browser.

20. Macro: A piece of computer code that is executed automatically when another piece of code is triggered by the user, such as by using hotkeys in a word processing program or by pressing a button on a mouse. Certain operating systems include macro features (e.g., Microsoft Office, Apple iTunes, Mac OS X). Macros are used in computer-aided design (CAD) software to automate repetitive tasks in the software, requiring fewer mouse movements or keystrokes.

CHAPTER 2:

WHAT EXACTLY IS A PROGRAMMING LANGUAGE?

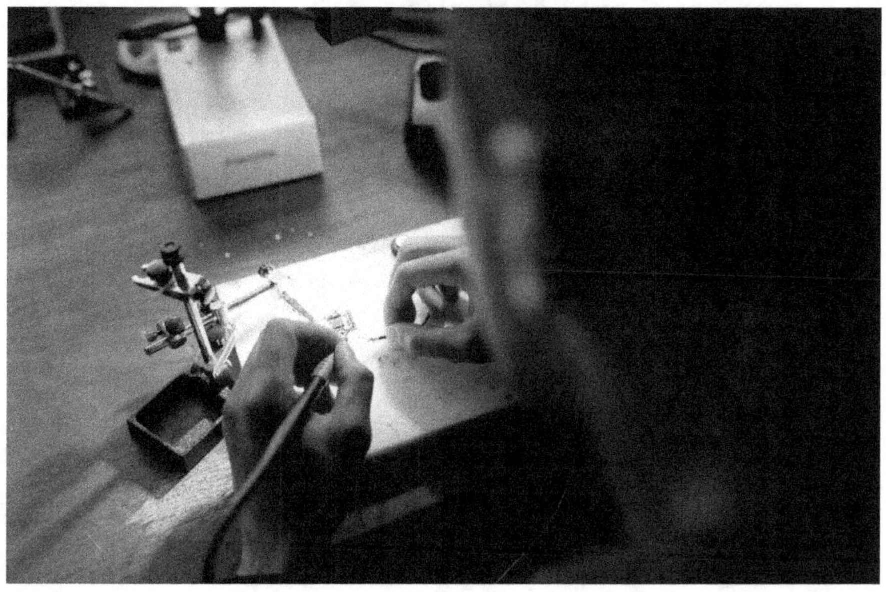

The first thing you should know is that a programming language is a set of computer instructions. These are frequently referred to as code. The goal is to get computers to do what they need to do, which can range from creating calculators to processing NASA images of nearby galaxies. The difficult part about programming languages is that they are frequently not designed for people who do not already know how to code. It's the equivalent of attempting to teach someone Spanish in a first-grade class. The majority of people will not understand what you're saying. As a result, this book is intended for complete beginners who have no prior experience with programming languages. It doesn't matter how much experience you have in other languages; you'll still need basic computer knowledge to pick up and use this language effectively. (If you want to learn more about these topics, check out my other web development books.)

What Exactly Is Coding?

Consider code to be instructions that tell the computer what to do. If I tell the computer to "draw a picture," it will do so on the screen. The laptop has a lot of programming power, including the ability to understand instructions. It may need to interpret one or two of them, but for the most part, it will be able to follow these instructions and do what you ask.

What Motivates Us to Code?

Software is created using programming languages. Software is essential because it enables us to do things like automate factory processes or connect devices in our homes to control them from anywhere in the world. This type of software is commonly referred to as "apps," which is an abbreviation for applications.

So coding is necessary because it allows us to create our own apps to help us do what we want. But coding is about more than just the language: it's about what you can do with it. Coding is also a creative process, which is where all of the best apps come from from. Apps that are useful, interesting, or simply entertaining to use are more likely to be successful. Some have changed the way we live our lives, such as Uber or Facebook, while others, such as Skype or WhatsApp, have had a significant impact on how we communicate with one another. And they were all made possible because someone had an idea and was able to translate it into code somewhere.

What Are You Going to Do With It?

Anything comes to mind. Coding allows you to create something from nothing. You give it a few lines of code, and it transforms into a program that does something on your computer, your network, or even the World Wide Web.

You might believe that all coding is the same, but there are several types. Simple websites are built using coding languages. Others are used to create operating systems, which complicate matters. Some people learn how to code in high school or college in order to write programs for large corporations such as Google and Microsoft; others learn how to code for themselves or their friends in order to create software on a shoestring budget.

This book will teach you how to create software for your computer using Python, a popular programming language. This is an excellent language to learn because there are numerous resources available. There are also many Python-based apps available so you can see how they work, play with them, and even copy them to use in your own projects.

Some of these websites and apps may appear to be expensive or require specialized equipment, but all you need is a computer. And, for the time being, all you need to learn to code is a computer with an internet connection and the ability to read, type, and do simple math.

This Book's Reading Procedure

Programming is a difficult subject. Even if you're completely new to computers, chances are you already know at least a few programming languages. That's why I wrote this book: I want people who have never coded before to understand what they're reading. The following are the steps you must take in order to use this book:

1. If you haven't already, download and install Python 2 on your computer. (Python 3 is very similar to Python 2, and many of the examples will work with either version.)

2. Launch a web browser and navigate to https://codecademy.com/courses/learn-python?action=start.

3. Continue reading the chapters as you go. You must enter the code and then follow the instructions for each chapter. (If no code or instructions appear, click "Start a new lesson.")

4. Read this book all the way through. You'll want to put what you've learned into practice so that it sticks in your mind!

Where to Find Out More

After finishing this book, you'll want to learn more about Python and coding. Here are some resources that I think you should check out: – Codecademy Codecademy is a fun website where you can learn to code in a variety of languages, including Python, by completing activities and challenges on their platform. There are even video tutorials!

Codecademy is a fun website where you can learn to code in a variety of languages, including Python, by completing activities and challenges on their platform. There are even video tutorials! Udacity.

This is similar to Codecademy, except that it is a college-level course and the program you learn here can be applied to almost any job. There are also numerous videos on the site that demonstrate how the modules work and how to use them. Books and YouTube are two excellent resources for learning, and they are both free! Many books and online courses are available to help you learn Python. You can also lookup Python videos on YouTube to see how other people have used it in their projects.

CHAPTER 3:

WHY DO WE NEED A PROGRAMMING LANGUAGE?

A computer's most common use is to store and retrieve data. Computers can read data from memory chips and convert it to text, video, or any other format that we can view. They, on the other hand, are unable to comprehend or process the information itself—it is simply a collection of electronic impulses. So, what does this imply? It means that it requires us, humans, to tell it what to do in order for the computer to function at all.

Now, programming languages come in handy because they allow us, as humans, to instruct computers on how to process the data we store on them. Yes, we will need to know how to write a program that instructs the computer on what to do. However, if we want the computer to do anything, we cannot write a program by hand! Computers can only operate in eight modes and understand only English or binary code.

As a result, we require a method for computers to understand and process all types of human languages. Programming languages have been developed so that anyone with little or no experience can write programs ranging from simple webpages and word processors to complex games such as Quake III Arena and World of Warcraft. It is the same language used in chat rooms and music players on our computers, as well as mobile phones and digital cameras. If you want to go beyond simply writing small programs for your own use, you'll need to learn how to program in order to create the software that allows all of this to happen.

How do you explain coding to a child?

Programming is the process of deciding what data the computer should process in order to achieve the desired result. There are many different types of programming languages, some more complex than others, but they all have something in common. They all require us to select a set of instructions that tell the computer exactly how to operate. It appears to be simple—and it is!

Consider the following example: You've just purchased an iPod and want to use iTunes to play music from your computer. You have a couple of songs on your computer's hard drive that you want to play on your iPod. How do you instruct iTunes to perform this action? Isn't it as simple as plugging in the iPod and selecting it from the iTunes menu? That works, but you might want to consider what is going on here. If all we know is that we need iTunes to transfer songs to our iPod, why aren't we just connecting our computer directly via USB?

21

We can see some decisions we need to make if we think like a programmer here. First and foremost, we must determine which songs will be transferred. Second, we must inform iTunes that those are the songs we want it to transfer over. Third, iTunes needs to know whether we want them transferred to an iPod or a computer.

How do you go about doing this? iTunes, on the other hand, is a relatively simple program that the user can easily control with a few mouse clicks. However, beneath this simple interface is a slightly more complex set of instructions that tell iTunes exactly how to function. This is what programming languages do for computers: they allow us to type out the instructions, which are then translated into commands that the computer can understand and process.

What's It Like to Code?

Programming is more than just typing in a bunch of random numbers and letters. Instead, it can be compared to putting together a puzzle. You're trying to figure out how to tell the computer what you want it to do without knowing how it all works — it's like solving a puzzle!

So, what are some examples of coding issues you might encounter? Computers, on the other hand, use various types of data that they must process in accordance with their programming language. Some computers, for example, will have simple graphical user interfaces (GUIs) whose sole purpose is to draw pictures or read information from files on your hard disk. These computers will not recognize commands entered into a text editor or even an email application. Other computers are more akin to an old typewriter in that they have a user interface, but it is at a low level and cannot understand anything other than text. You can instruct these computers to type information for you, but they will only understand the text you typed in.

So, in the case of our iPod, if you tried to transfer your songs using a GUI-based computer, it wouldn't be able to tell which songs you wanted to move. And if you told an older computer that relied on text commands what type of file was on your hard drive, it would not know how to operate. The key point here is that code can only go so far as to understand and work with the required data.

So, what motivates you to use a computer? As I previously stated, computers are capable of performing many tasks that we are not. In some ways, programming is similar to playing chess and designing your pieces and thinking ahead by the end of the game — and it's an amazing experience.

How does it feel to code? Every day, you write new code! There is, however, a learning curve, as with most things in life.

The more you code, the less difficult it becomes.

By experimenting with various options, you will begin to gain an understanding of what is possible and what works best. So, while you may have some difficulty understanding how things work at first, you will gradually gain a better understanding of how computers work. If this sounds like something you'd be interested in, coding could be the career for you!

CHAPTER 4:

POPULAR PROGRAMMING LANGUAGES

The most widely used programming languages in the world today. Java, Python, PHP, C/C++, and Ruby are among them. This book compares these languages and delves into the key differences between them. This book concludes with a conclusion to help readers decide which language to learn. The author also recommends courses that can be used to learn these programming languages online without having to purchase any textbooks or other materials.

This provides many useful resources for people interested in learning new skills and learning more about popular programming languages. The book is lengthy, but it provides a practical guide to deciding which programming languages to learn first. Knowing how to program can provide many advantages, such as the flexibility of finding a job in programming. You will also be able to earn more money because you will have more control over your career and how much you are paid for it.

This section of the book compares Java, Python, PHP, and Ruby in terms of popularity, websites built with those languages, and the ability to develop mobile apps for Google Android or Apple iOS. You can browse through an extremely long list of websites created with these programming languages to find many useful sites.

This section of the book compares C and C++ programming languages. It is based on quotes from programmers who prefer one language over another. It also describes strategies used by businesses and institutions to improve their business applications through the use of one or both programming languages.

This section of the book will teach you how to use Python for a variety of purposes. First, you'll learn how to use Python for web development and which website platforms are supported. The author also provides a few different ways to obtain Python, such as downloading directly from the Python website.

This section of the book examines five of the best programming textbooks and provides readers with information on each of them. You will find abstracts for each textbook, which is extremely useful if you are unsure which book to purchase first. It also provides helpful hints for locating additional books at a local library or through online retailers such as Amazon or eBay.

This section of the book compares PHP and Ruby on Rails in great detail. You will find quotes from famous programmers and CEOs who were asked about their experience with these programming languages.

This section of the book includes a performance evaluation of several popular programming languages. There is a variety of

Python, Ruby, Java, and C# tests available. If you have any questions about the test, the author provides a helpful set of instructions that you can use to perform it yourself.

This section of the book compares Java and Android. It is based on quotes from programmers who prefer one language over another. The book also describes strategies used by businesses and institutions to improve their business applications through the use of one or both of these programming languages.

CHAPTER 5:

UNDERSTANDING A PROGRAM'S STRUCTURE

This section of the book aims to get you started quickly with coding basics, teaching you the first step: understanding the structure of a program.

The Program's Organization

In our case, we have a program that prints hello and goodbye. The syntax indicates that we will create two distinct functions, each with its own data and logic. Because it has separate procedures that can be executed at any time and in any order, it is often referred to as procedural programming.

Variables in Programming: An Overview

Every programming language, as previously stated, has its own set of rules and quirks, but they all have one thing in common: variables.

Types of Variable Data

Data types specify how values are stored in variables. The variables used in the preceding example are integer and string. Each one represents a particular value or a bit sequence of bits. Integers are represented by int, while the text is represented by a string. Aside from the data type, each variable has its own value that can be changed by the programmer when run through the computer's compiler. As an illustration:

$$1 + 23 + 4 = 27.56$$

When you add 23 and 4.5, you get 27.6, but we store it in a variable rather than as 27. It's the same as having one dollar and saying, "I have one dollar," except you'd say "$1" instead of "one dollar." Please keep in mind that each programming language has its own terminology for variables such as int, string, float, and so on.

In our next tutorial, we'll learn how to manipulate variables in greater depth.

Understanding a Program's Structure: Function of a Subroutine Because it has separate procedures that can be executed at any time and in any order, our example above is known as procedural programming. In this example, the primary function is the first to be executed. This is the start of our program, also known as the primary procedure in programming jargon. The program can invoke a series of subroutines (functions), which are then executed at any time. Each process has its own set of values and logic that can be used by itself or in conjunction with other functions.

Logic & Commands

Commands are used to instruct the interpreter (computer) on how to run our program. Commands are the specific instructions you give your program to manage. Print, input, if, else, and while are all common programming commands.

Logic is used in addition to instructions. Sense instructs the computer to carry out a specific command based on a set of conditions. For example, we can use the if knowledge to check certain conditions and instruct the interpreter (computer) to perform one or more actions.

Understanding a Program's Structure: Data Assessor

In our example, we have the main function that can invoke a number of subroutines. These are known as data assessors because they provide answers to the question, "What is this variable?" A data assessor functions as an entry point into your program, assisting you in responding to this variable. There should be one and only one data accessor for each variable in your program. Your program will not run correctly if you create two or more variables with their own separate data accessors.

Programming Weirdnesses and Hints

There are a few peculiarities to be aware of as you begin programming. For example, if you want to write a program that asks the user for their name, don't use quotes around the user's name. This is due to the fact that every variable must begin with a letter or an underscore ( ). As a result, "Alice" will not work because it is interpreted as Alice, which is not a valid variable. You should use "username" if you need to ask the user for their name. The underscore character (_) is used to separate variables so that they do not get mixed up. There is also a concept known as scope. This is a fundamental concept that you are most likely already aware of. Our program can use the scope to determine which variables are defined in the program and where they are defined. Because their position determines this, the first variable on any line of code is known as the local scope and can be accessed without having to write out the variable's name. However, if you start printing variables outside of your subroutines, you will need to write their names down.

Terminology in Programming

Classes, Objects, Variables, and Functions are all types of data.

The object-oriented programming methodology allows you to store data in your computer programs in a more structured and orderly manner. Object-oriented programming is similar to what we learn in high school and college, but it is applied differently in practice. This methodology generates classes of objects that are intended to resemble real-world objects.

A class is a way to organize your program into groups with similar values, methods or actions (functions), and properties. The term "class" is derived from a set of values known as attributes. The attributes can range from numbers to strings or built-in variables like location, size, speed, time, and so on. In our previous program, we have one class called main with one attribute called EXE. The EXE variable, in other words, is defined in the program.

We can make objects that inherit from a class by creating one. In our program, for example, we created a class called "Main" that inherits from the "Main" class. Using this class, we can then create an object called main (it will be called main).

A variable is similar to any other variable in your program, with the exception that it can be used by multiple classes/objects and has its own scope. Variables defined outside of subroutines are referred to as global variables, as opposed to variables defined within subroutines. Variables defined in the same class all have the same scope, meaning they can be accessed at any time within that class. The variable scope is determined by where the variable is defined (local or global scope), but once a variable is defined (local or global scope), it always has a scope.

CHAPTER 6:

DIFFERENT PROGRAM TYPES

Let's take a look at the various types of programs and see which ones might be best for each level of experience.

Where Should You Study Coding? Many people are unaware that coding can be learned in a variety of ways.

If you're new to programming, a language like Python or Java is a great place to start. These languages are simpler for beginners to learn because they do not require prior knowledge of any other programming language. You'll probably want to try your hand at C++ or PHP once you've mastered these two languages (or something else entirely).

If you've already learned one or more programming languages and want to try something new, you should probably try a new language that takes a different approach than the ones you already know. As a result, C++ and Java may be a good place to start. These languages are similar enough to others that transitioning from them should be relatively simple (once you know another language).

If you're already a seasoned programmer, there's no need to upgrade your current development environment. However, it can still be beneficial to switch over to Js for a short period of time to become acquainted with a different approach. Once this is accomplished, learning other languages will be much easier for you in the future.

Knowledge of the Internet: If you're new to programming, you should make sure you understand how the internet works before embarking on your new adventure. Although it may appear intimidating at first, the internet isn't that difficult to grasp.

It may not be necessary for you to learn HTML and CSS before you begin learning web development (after all, they are fairly simple languages), but it will be beneficial if you do.

Discover the Internet:

Don't Put Off Learning To Code: The best time to start is right now. It makes no difference if you're 100 years old, ten years old, or somewhere in between. Who can learn how things work is not limited. You can learn how things work if you know how to read. If you are ready to begin learning programming languages, or if you have already begun, then pick up one of the books listed above and begin your journey into the world of coding.

This does not imply that the rest of the journey will be easy.

There will always be new challenges ahead, but if learning to code is something that interests you, the journey will be worthwhile. More people learning how things work is the best way to make things more accessible. The more people who know how to code there are, the easier it will be to learn. So, what are you holding out for?

CHAPTER 7:

HOW DOES A PROGRAM GET CREATED?

There are several approaches to developing a program, but in this beginner's guide, we will concentrate on one: top-down design.

Top-down design is a programming method in which the highest-level modules are designed first, followed by lower-level modules based on these high-level modules. This method is ideal for beginners because it allows them to easily divide their program into logical sections.

Step One: Create a Program Plan

Before you begin, you must have a clear idea of what your program should accomplish. You might want to consider things like

35

your program's input and output, as well as the data it will process. It's time to get started once you believe you have a good idea!

Step 2: Designing Your Program's Data Structure

The first step will be to design our data structure. In this case, we'll make use of an array. This array will contain three numbers: a list of integers and two floating-point numbers. These will be some user input that we will process later in our program.

Step 3: Create the Main Program Loop

Now that we've decided where to store the data and what our program should do, it's time to create the main program loop (also known as the main function).

Step 4: Create the Processors

The processors are a series of functions that will be executed in order.

These processors receive data and perform operations on it, such as adding or subtracting numbers or converting bytes to integers.

Step 5:

Constructing the Final Program Loop We can now construct our final program loop now that we've seen what the processors should do (also known as the main function). You will have a C++ program that looks like this when you are finished writing it:

int main #include stdio.h> ()

Step 6: Designing a Data Structure

We need to create our data structure now that we have the main program loop. This is simply because we kept track of our data from the previous step:

main int ()

Step 7: Create the Processors

Now that we've built our data structure, we can start working on the processors. The first processor should take user input and convert it to an integer that will be added to the list of integers. To begin, you should write your first processor function. This will be referred to as convert to integer ().

Because you'll be receiving user input, you'll need an if statement to ensure that the data is a number.

Step 8: Create the Final Program Loop

Now that we've created our convert to integer() processor function, we can include it in the main program loop.

It's time to write your next processor function now that you've added convert to integer() to your main program loop. This will be known as add numbers ().

You'll need another if statement (or else statement) inside your new add numbers() processor function because you should only add numbers and not convert integers to floating-point numbers.

Step 9: Create the Final Program Loop

Now that you've created your add numbers() processor function, you can incorporate it into your main program loop.

The final processor's name will be display numbers (). Let's get started with this program, which will output the number list and the sum. You'll want to make sure the user has entered at least two numbers because they won't be able to add anything if they don't.

Step 10: Design a data structure.

Now that we've finished our final program loop, let's build a data structure. This will save our list of numbers as well as our sum so that we can output them later.

Save and compile your program. If there are no errors, your program should be ready to run!

The user's first step will be to enter some data to ensure that they can. When the user runs our program, he or she will see a prompt asking for some information. When they enter a number, we will save it to an array and then prompt them for another. This procedure will be repeated until the user enters zero or a negative number.

Step 11: Create the Final Program Loop

We're ready to build our final program loop now that we've confirmed that the user entered numbers (also known as the main function).

When a user enters data into our processor, we assign that data to our list of integers and then add all of those numbers together.

Finally, let us output the array of numbers and the sum to ensure that everything worked properly.

Appendix C: Simple C++ Programming Hints

Coding is enjoyable, but it can also be frustrating. While you may be tempted to throw in the towel and start over, there are a few things you can do to alleviate your programming woes. We've saved the best for last, so let's get started!

Coding Help Is Your Best Friend

It makes no difference if your program works. If it's impossible for anyone to use it, it's not a good program. Consider how many times people have been let down by programs that they thought would help them but turned out to be ineffective.

CHAPTER 8:

HOW IS A PROGRAM PUT INTO ACTION?

The first step in developing any program is translating it from the original programming language (usually C++ or Java) into machine code (zeros and ones). This is accomplished by a program known as the compiler.

A program always begins with "statements" or "instructions," which instruct the computer on what to do, either sequentially or in parallel (i.e., by doing them at the same time). For example, if you want the program to print "Hello" followed by "World," you would tell it: print("Hello") print("World")

This is written in machine code as:

0x420000 Hello there, 0x420001. 0x420002 in the world

Where "0x" is a hexadecimal number (the kind used in computers to describe numbers). This diagram depicts how each line of code is divided into instructions. Each instruction is disguised as a single letter of the alphabet in order for the computer to understand what to do with it. (This is known as "coding.")

BASIC (which stands for "Beginner's All-purpose Symbolic Instruction Code") was created to be as simple to learn as possible for those who had never programmed before. Each line of code is written with only a few characters that can be typed on a standard keyboard. BASIC has been around since the late 1950s and is still used today by programming hobbyists as well as in many schools to introduce programming languages in general. You don't need any special equipment or software to learn about or experiment with BASIC programs.

The most basic BASIC programs are written using a few keywords from the original version of the language, which was developed in the 1960s; they are:

PRINT: Displays a single line of text on the screen. STORE: This function stores a number in a variable (a name for an area of memory) READ: This command reads a line of text from the keyboard. INTO: Stores or prints a single value derived from multiple numbers and/or variables. LOOP: Recursively executes the next line of code until something true is no longer true. GOTO: Navigates to another section of code (instrumental when writing programs) END: Terminates the program.

These keywords are combined to form a complete program. The program below, for example, prints the text "Hello World" on the screen, followed by a number between 0 and 10: 10 PRINT "Hello World" 20 INPUT n 30 IF n0 THEN 80 40 PRINT n 50 GOTO 30 80 END

The first line instructs the computer to begin reading instructions at the beginning of the next line. As a result, the computer processes the second line (#10). As in the previous "Hello World" program, the number is prefixed with an apostrophe once more. This is done so that the computer recognizes the line as a number.

The third line (#20) instructs the computer what to do if it encounters a "conditional" statement, which is used to ensure that something is true before proceeding with whatever follows it. In this case, it determines whether the user has pressed any keys on their keyboard. If they pressed a key, the computer will process whatever is between the brackets (the lines below). If not, the computer will continue with the remainder of line #20.

The fourth line (#30) checks to see if the number after it is less than zero (i.e., it has a "negative sign"). If this is the case, it returns to line #80. Everything will be repeated here as long as the number is negative.

As a result, the fourth line (#30) instructs the computer to repeat whatever it sees before this point in the program until it sees a bar labeled "End." If you wanted the computer to continue until it encountered a "Stop" or "End," which could be used for debugging, you would type:

```
30 IF n0 THEN 80 40 PRINT n 50 GOTO 30 80 END
```

This is referred to as a "looping" program. It means that whatever happens over and over again. If you print everything when you step through this loop (by pressing the "Enter" key), it should look like this:

As these examples demonstrate, there are numerous approaches to writing BASIC programs. There are two ways to write the line (#30), which checks whether the number is less than zero.

30 IF n=0, THEN 80

This is one method that employs a single line "IF" statement. The alternative method, which uses two lines to write the same statement, is as follows:

GOTO 80 IF n0THEN 30

The computer is programmed to read the line by row, beginning at the beginning of each line of code. This means that when it comes across the "THEN," it will stop reading that line and continue with whatever follows. Because of this, the two ways of writing this statement are referred to as different programming languages: BASIC and Visual Basic.

"Hello World" PRINT "Hello, World!" PRINT END PRINT "Hello, World" A previous question about programs like this was why we needed to put line numbers after the first line. The program, as you can see, is designed to read each line of code from left to right. As a result, the computer can read the lines in any order it desires. Line numbers are frequently used by programmers to identify where they are in the overall program.

Textboxes

Most Visual Basic programs will have a large number of lines of code. You may want to refer to a specific line or mean something specific within the program at times. For example, you might want to return to a specific section of the program or display a list of some kind. Textboxes are one method for accomplishing this. They enable you to write text as if it were code and then access it later with commands such as "PRINT", "PRINTA", and so on, as described above.

CHAPTER 9:

PROGRAM STATEMENTS

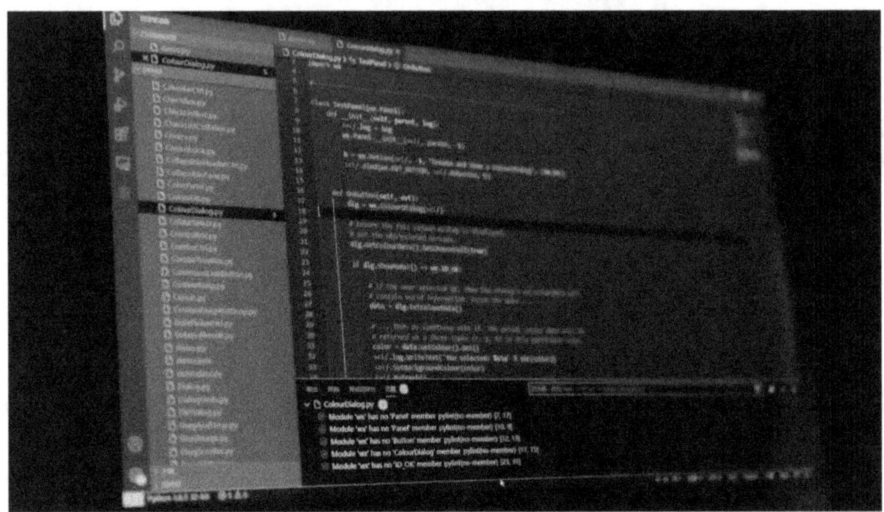

Individual instructions that you, as the programmer, give to your computer are referred to as program statements.

A programming language is frequently used to write code. A programming language is a collection of symbols and rules that are used to create commands that computers can execute. Each line of code in a program statement must be spaced out with one space between each word and wrapped at 80 characters in order for humans and machines to read the code.

We've all experienced the frustration of wanting to do something but not knowing how or where to begin. I'll start from scratch, explaining everything you need to know to create your programs. I'll walk you through the steps of writing, compiling, and running a program. Each section will teach you a new skill that will build on previous knowledge and skills, giving you a better understanding of programming.

I want to make programming accessible to newcomers like myself! You see, I started my first programming course at university with no prior coding experience at all. I had no idea what the lecturer was on about or how he expected us to complete our assignments. This annoyance prompted me to embark on a quest to learn how others were taught to program or how they learned on their own, as well as the challenges they encountered. I discovered that many people began learning on their own as well, but they quickly became discouraged and hit a difficult roadblock. This is the obstacle I'm here to help you overcome.

So let's get started!

What exactly is a program?

A computer program, like any other list, is simply a set of instructions for the computer to follow. Shopping lists, day-to-day tasks, and even schoolwork all have one thing in common: they're all lists of things to do. These instructions are referred to as "statements," and each statement in your program will assist in instructing the computer on how to complete your task.

Some statements are simple, such as writing one letter to the screen, whereas others are more complex and include many things happening at the same time!

Our main program will be called 'Program.BAS,' so it must have a distinct name. It must also be saved in the 'Videos' folder, with the file extension '.BAS.' You won't be able to run your program unless you have this.

All of these factors must be in sync for your program to run correctly or at all. So, if you're having trouble with this section, please double-check that you've done everything correctly.

This is how we should organize our folders:

45

Codey v1.0 is a Windows program. This means that the program can only be run on Windows computers, and you must have the necessary software to run it. Linux users may believe they are exempt from these rules, but this is a Windows-only tutorial, so please adhere to them!

Important: If you are using a Mac, the app will most likely not work properly. There are numerous programs that are incompatible with Mac OS X.

What Exactly Is Coding?

Many factors contribute to the creation of a computer program, which we refer to as a program "encoding Coding isn't only what you're doing now. It is the process of translating a program from your head into something that a computer can understand.

All of this coding will be done in a programming language such as Python, C#, C++, or Basic — there are thousands of different languages, each with its own set of features.

Our program will be written in Microsoft's BASIC programming language, which is easy to learn and a good place to start if you've never done it before.

If you know how to code in another language, this tutorial is unlikely to teach you anything new.

Statements of Program

When you write a program, you are essentially writing individual commands for the computer to execute. These lines of code will be written one at a time. A program statement is analogous to a sentence in a speech. If the speaker were to write

46

this down on their phone, it would be "I will go to the store and buy some bread."

Statements frequently contain multiple instructions at the same time. These instructions are executed in the order listed, so if we wanted to tell our computer to "Buy some bread," we'd write it like this: I want you to all take note of how many spaces separate each instruction and how many characters are in each education. Take note of how that statement is wrapped onto a new line, as well as how the instruction is 80 characters long. If you're writing your code in another program, this may not apply to you - just write it so that humans can read it and the computer can run it properly.

Structure of the language

Let's take a look at how our BASIC programming language works now that we've defined what a program statement is.

Syntax tells the computer exactly how we want our program to be written, what syntax to use, and where/how to space everything out. It also indicates where each instruction starts and ends.

Program statements are simply programs in and of themselves. They may instruct the computer to execute additional statements in our program or instruct the computer to perform some action. Each instruction will instruct the computer to perform a specific action, similar to how a sentence has different words for different situations.

All of our program's commands will be enclosed by these brackets,

Brackets simply contain everything for our program, so anything written within them will be read and acted upon by the computer.

What should go here in terms of statements?

So, what goes in the spaces between the brackets? Each line of code can contain one or more statements, and each statement operates independently of the others. If you remove one of your statements, the program will continue to run normally.

You can't run any of your programs unless you have program statements.

As long as you follow the rules, programming languages allow you to format your code however you want. Add more code between those brackets if you want to add more instructions or a conditional statement! However, the computer will ignore it, so don't worry too much about it - go ahead and write that "WHAT IF...

CHAPTER 10:

DATA TYPES, VARIABLES, AND OPERATORS

Data Types: Variables and Operators are two of the three fundamental programming components that will help you learn how to code. This book will go over data types, variables, and operators, with an emphasis on the fundamentals. Variables are containers for storing data (such as numbers), whereas Operators are used to performing actions on that data. Data types assist you in managing your program's memory usage by informing it of the types of things it can store.

Variables:

In your program, a variable is a container for storing information (such as numbers). In memory, the computer stores various types of information about your program and its environments, such as warehouses or storage areas. When your program requires that information, it requests it from the computer.

Operators: An operator is a programming symbol that changes how a value is used in your program. For example, the symbol = indicates that you are assigning a number to an existing variable. The equals sign can be used as an assignment operator as well. 15 = 15 instructs the computer to assign the number 15 to the variable named 15.

The Key Ideas: We must now discuss what variables are for and how they work. The computer will use a certain amount of memory for your program, and if left alone, it will continue to use that memory until you tell it to stop. When this occurs, your program will not function properly. The computer will not save all of the information about your actions in the program. So, how do you notify the computer that you require additional memory?

The Basic Rule: Create variables (or store data in variables) first, then use them in your programs! This may appear to be a little contradictory.

. This means that you write code to handle all of the information in your program, and when it needs to find a new piece of memory for your program, you tell it where to look. You must understand data types in order for this process to work.

Data Types: When you create a variable, you are telling the computer how much memory it needs and what type of data it can store. This informs the computer that if the variable contains information, it will know exactly how to access it and display it on your screen (or do other things). Without this data, the computer will be unable to understand what you want it to do and will be forced to shut down.

Consider the following scenario: you own a clothing store. You decide to use an inventory system that counts how many different types of clothing you have in stock because you sell clothes. You can imagine your inventory system as a large shelf with many other boxes scattered around it, all filled with clothes. If your program requires clothing, it can go to the shelf, grab a box, and return it to the dressing room for someone to try it on. These boxes function similarly to variables in that they store information about lists of things in the world (like your stock of clothes).

Data Types are Not the Same: There is a significant difference between these variable boxes and the inventory sheets of paper. Each of these boxes has a place to label what it contains. However, there is no way to know what is inside the box without opening it and inspecting it for yourself. If you want the computer to know that box 1 contains dresses, your program must open that box, examine the label you added, and determine what became your clothes when you opened the box.

Put a + sign in front of a variable to tell the computer what data type it is (these signs are called prefixes because they come before other signs or symbols). Each box in your inventory system should have a label that tells you what's inside. The computer will recognize the + sign and use it to determine the type of clothing you have in each box (this process is called data typing). The boxes are variables in programming. By adding a prefix, the variable becomes data typed, indicating that the computer understands how to use that variable.

Here's an illustration: In your program, you're using a variable called bob, and you want the computer to know that this variable contains employees. Then you'd type bob+, which stands for employee. You can make as many variables as you want by replacing bob+ with a different word, such as clerk+ or cashier+. Because you did this, the computer now recognizes Bob as an employee. It has no idea what it is holding at this point, only that bob contains individual employees and that it can display these employees in your program in the same way that clothing or any other type of inventory is displayed.

A - sign in front of a variable's name is another way to tell it what kind of information it can hold. This informs the computer that the variable can store any data (called general). Assume you are a teacher with a large number of grades to assign in your program. You can create a variable called grades+ that will allow your program to take any type of grade, print it out on the screen, and then append an appropriate + sign to it. This is how a computer interprets a standard letter grade, such as B+.

Prefixes are special symbols that appear before other signs or symbols. While these do not directly tell the computer what type of information is stored in the variables, they do tell the computer what it can do with it.

CHAPTER 11:

THE IMPORTANCE OF STRINGS

There are many different types of computer programming languages for writing programs that communicate with one another. Some programming languages make use of keywords and numbers, while others make use of symbols and a combination of the two, and still, others make extensive use of strings.

The string type is useful because it can represent any type of detailed element in any graphical interface. In Python, for example, the command "Move ten meters East" would look like this: "move('10m','E')". The Python text editor, as you are aware, is simple. All it needs to figure out is how to move something.

You would probably not want to use numbers if you were writing a program that could be used to manipulate some aspect of the user interface. You'd need a way to tell your program which buttons to press or which coordinates a mouse movement should correspond to. And, in order for a command string like "Move ten meters East" or anything else to be useful, the information contained within it must be stored somewhere and associated with some other type of entity.

Strings come in handy here because they can store any amount of information that can be transmitted between two applications. Our "Move ten meters East" command would be written as follows:

move('10m','E')

If a program, such as the Python editor, requests a list of coordinates or button commands, all it has to do is create a string with each element in the list. This way, when reading an element from a string, you can treat it exactly like any other array entry.

When it comes to using strings for commands and data, having only one type of information stored in them can be very limiting, especially if you intend to send strings thousands or millions of miles between devices. This is where the concept of "encoding" comes into play.

Encoding is the process of converting the content of a string into a format that a computer can use more efficiently for sending and storage. This simple example will help you understand how encoding works.

Assume there is an application that has been programmed to send the command "Save all data" to all of the devices in the Earth's environment. This command would be sent by an application that looks like this:

```
>>> s.encode('UTF8') >>> here(s = 'Save all data.') >>> save+all+data print(s)
```

One of the most important aspects of encoding is that it occurs in both directions. An encoded string must first be decoded before it can be sent anywhere. In other words, in order for our above-mentioned application to be able to execute the command "Save all data.", it must be able to receive and decode a string like the one we've created here:

save'everything'

The second important thing to understand is that encodings have names, and the encoding we used above has the name UTF-8. Encoding is similar to a programming language in that it has a name, an interpreter, and can be used to communicate with other entities.

Now that you understand how encodings work and how strings are used to represent commands, let's look at how we can use a string to interpret the command "Save all data." in Python.

Translation: Convert our string "Save all data." to an ASCII string, then decode it so it can be used as a command. Because Python 3 uses ASCII encoding, which converts strings to uppercase letters, we must first convert the string to ASCII format.

Remember that strings can contain any number of text fragments, so we must ensure that our command only contains letters or digits in order for it to be correctly understood. Once we have the ASCII string, we must convert it to a command.

We will always use a "private" string referring to the encoding to ensure that our strings can be easily converted and decoded. Let's take another look at that code:

```
>>> here(s = 'Save all data.') >>> s.encode('UTF8') >>> Print(s)
Save+all+data. Save all data with s.decode().
```

If we go through this code step by step, you'll notice that the first time it runs, it converts a Python string into an ASCII string and then decodes the ASCII string into a Python object called a'string.' Then it can be used in the same way as any other command.

The next time, we can simply use the string object's "encode" method to convert the string into a UTF-8 Python string for saving all data. In addition to the convert between ASCII and UTF-8 that we used in this exercise, strings have methods that can be used to convert between multiple different encodings. Consider the following example:

>>> here(s = 'ananas') >>> s.encode('UTF8') ananas print(s) >>> >>> s.decode() ananas ananas.encode('ASCII')

The final thing you should know about encoding is that Python supports a variety of encodings, which are defined by the variable "encoding." These are the encodings:

ASCII = 'ASCII'

latin1 = iso 8859 1.

utf 8 is equivalent to 'utf-8'.

Now that you've learned everything there is to know about encoding, let's look at how we can apply what we've learned to make our own program more efficient when sending and receiving strings. Take a look at the following information:

data = ['test,"joke,"name]

56

```python
print('All',data,'of',len(data),'with',len(data),'no',len(data),'ne
wlines.')
```

The code above determines the length of a list and outputs it in a variety of ways. So, what's the big deal here? So, how many lines of output would we get if we added one more item to our list? Let us investigate. Here's what we'll do: add one more item to our list before running the code above. The code is as follows:

```python
data = ['test,"joke,"name,'newline]
```

```python
print('All',data,'of',len(data),'with',len(data),'no',len(data),'ne
wlines.')
```

We get the following results: 4 out of 5 with 0 newlines. If you're paying attention, you'll notice that we now have one more line than before. This is because the list was empty and so when it printed len(data) , it added a new line because newlines aren't allowed in Python, but they are allowed in some programming languages such as C++.

CHAPTER 12:

ITERATIVE PROGRAMMING

Iterative programming is an effective method for moving from vague, undefined systems to more specific and refined ones through repeated development cycles. Typically, the process starts with a set of requirements that are then quickly and imperfectly implemented. The system is then evaluated and improved in order to meet or exceed the initial goal.

The process is repeated until the system reaches near-perfection in terms of its original specifications, at which point maintenance is called in to keep things running smoothly. This development style starts a cycle known as "iteration," which restarts after completion with a new set of requirements or objectives (hence "iterative"). It's ideal for software systems where conditions are constantly changing or being added as a product matures.

There are several iterations within the iteration (i.e., a hierarchy of iterations) that gradually add detail to the system. Building an iterative approach into an organization's development cycle typically necessitates planning ahead of time so that time can be set aside throughout the project to implement and evaluate each iteration; allowing for changes; defining what constitutes successful completion of an iteration as well as project completion, so that there are consistent goals at all levels; and providing structure in the form of a framework to communicate what the system does and does not do.

Iterative methods are typically intended to assist a team in developing a solution incrementally, in small increments, and interactively. This is in contrast to waterfall methodologies, which impose an entire solution in one go from the start.

Iterative methodologies are focused on "continuously improving" rather than "frequently shipping"; thus, the term "iterative" does not necessarily refer to the cyclical nature of the methodological approach, but rather on continuous improvement. In this context, the adjective "iterative" refers to the construction of systems as small modules that can be evaluated and improved incrementally. It is a method of delivering solutions in stages, allowing for a modular implementation.

The iterative approach is widely used in product design and development, especially in the computer industry. It is also applicable in project management and other fields. Projects can be planned with a short-term goal by applying the framework of an iteration to project management (or milestone). The project's major phases or iterations then add some critical functionality that users require in order for the system to be useful. The iterative approach in project management enables problems and issues to be spotted early on and allows planning for time contingencies. This is critical because it ensures that the deliverables from each iteration are practical and usable by end-users.

In a project environment with changing requirements, the iterative approach also works well. When project managers expect the end-user to dictate system functionality, they can plan on using an iterative approach. Furthermore, by outlining requirements at the start of each iteration, project managers can control how features are implemented and ensure they are coordinated with other features planned for future iterations.

The key to an effective iterative development process is identifying potential issues early on, allowing time and budget for corrective action, and not jeopardizing delivery dates. This is also important because it ensures that the deliverables from each iteration are practical and usable by end-users.

When planning an iteration, a project manager, for example, should consider the following issues:

This helps ensure that end-users value and can use the deliverables from each iteration. For example, if the requirements for a new feature change at the last minute, the team can adapt to meet the budget/schedule. This is critical because it ensures that the deliverables from each iteration are practical and usable by end-users.

Iterative development is also effective in a project environment with changing requirements. When project managers expect the end-user to dictate system functionality, they can plan on using an iterative approach. Furthermore, by outlining requirements at the start of each iteration, project managers can control how features are implemented and ensure they are coordinated with other features planned for future iterations.

The key to an effective iterative development process is identifying potential issues early on, allowing time and budget for corrective action, and ensuring that delivery dates are not jeopardized. This helps ensure that end-users value and can use the deliverables from each iteration.

Another technique for transitioning from vague, undefined systems to more specific and refined ones through repeated development cycles is software re-engineering. Typically, the process starts with a set of requirements that are then quickly and imperfectly implemented. The system is then evaluated and improved in order to meet or exceed the initial goal.

A "specification" or "requirements document" in software engineering is a standard document communicated to project stakeholders or "users" during planning and construction to ensure that the system conforms to some defined set of expectations. It establishes goals and objectives, defines the scope of functionality, generates design options, imposes constraints on functionality, and defines relationships with other systems for interaction purposes.

The process of transforming, improving, or redesigning a software system based on analysis and feedback that reveals opportunities to improve functionality, efficiency, or quality, or to respond to changes in the marketplace, is known as re-engineering. In particular, it is applied to software projects.

Rapid prototyping allows for an early rethinking of requirements (prioritization), scope, and architecture.

A spiral development process is used, in which specification documents are used as input for requirements engineering.

They are integrating design and testing, incorporating test-driven development (TDD) into the improvement cycle, and deploying on an early production system.

61

One of the more difficult aspects of re-engineering is decommissioning legacy systems, which are typically not more than a few years old, and replacing them with new or upgraded systems. As the project seeks to replace the old system, it should be determined what benefit each decision will provide and then addressed accordingly.

CHAPTER 13:

CODE LOGICAL GROUPING

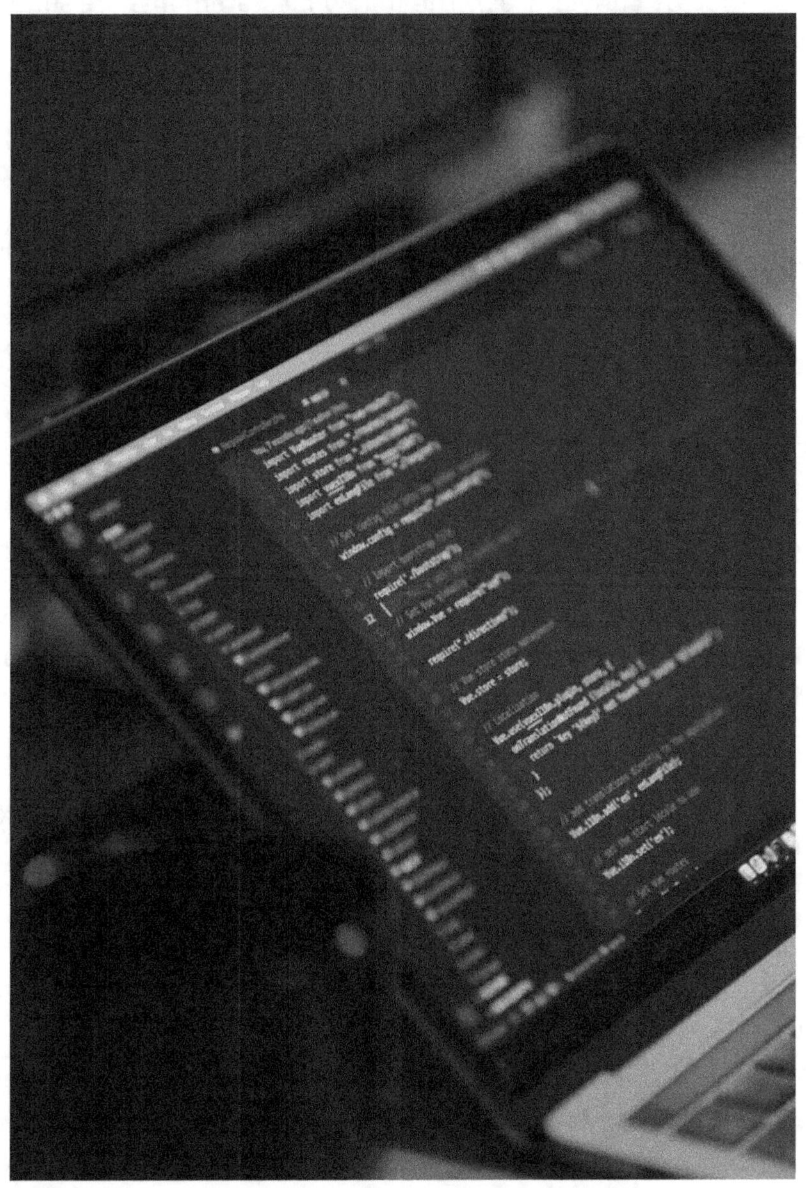

Java is a programming language with curly braces, semicolons, and a plethora of keywords. It is divided into logical groups of code. In Java, a "logical grouping of code" is a term used to describe a separate section of computer instructions (which are usually surrounded by curly braces). The following statements are suitable examples:

integer x = 1; integer y = 0; integer z = y * x

The statements in this section are used to demonstrate how multiple lines can exist within a single logical grouping. These specific examples do nothing more than set the values of variables (x,y, and z).

These lines of code should ideally be placed together because they are related to the same issue. Consider what would happen if we changed x to two and then y to nine:

integer x = 2; integer y = 9; integer z = y * x

There is some logic at work here. Instead of randomly assigning values for x and y (such as a=3 and b=9), the variable z will be equal to 18; there is a connection between them. This makes future code maintenance much easier when someone else has to try to make sense of what you did.

The only thing preventing you from writing code is your inability to read it. Don't be discouraged if it appears to be too complex or large to comprehend at first. Simply keep at it and learn by doing, and you'll get the hang of it!

It is critical to understand that good programmer do not write a lot of code during a project. They are much more concerned with the overall design of their program in order to gain a general understanding of what they are working on before writing the lines of code for it. A good programmer is willing to pause for a moment to consider the simplicity of what they are attempting, the possibilities, and whether there are much better ways of going about things. As a result, the code is better developed and there is a lot more flexibility when it comes to making changes.

The code should be written in smaller chunks that focus on a variety of topics. Smaller segments allow for more flexible coding, which can be used as a foundation for future projects and makes updates easier to implement later on. These segments should not become burdensome, as this would defeat the purpose of their creation in the first place.

When starting a new program, you must understand the fundamentals in order to build on them later. If you try to solve everything at the same time, you'll get stuck in a never-ending loop and never get anywhere. Begin by configuring some program parameters that will serve as a starting point (or a foundation) for your code.

Assume we want to write a program that will control the radio in our car based on its speed. We should be able to define a variable for controlling the speed of our radio and have it output that data back into the program on the computer screen.

"Let's see how things go" is a common phrase in programming. Instead of becoming frustrated, take your time and see if you can figure out what you need to do or solve the problem when it is presented to you. Code is designed to be worked with, and you should not feel obligated to do everything perfectly from the start.

It is preferable to take your time when attempting to solve a problem rather than rushing through it. However, there are times when we need the computer to wait for us to complete a task:

/ Do something while System.out.println("I'm Waiting").

The program that is currently running on our computer screen will pause its normal execution and wait for us to tell it what to do next.

Here's an example of how this might be applied: while (x!= 0) /do something x = x / 2; / System.out.println("I'm finished");

Because x equals 2 in the preceding program, we will divide it by 2 each time we run the loop (the while). This gives us a value of 1 for y, which is then assigned to a variable called z. Then, on your radio's display, use z to control the frequency.

Please see Java for Absolute Beginners and Coding for Absolute Beginners for more information.

A program is divided into three sections: input, transformation, and output (or simply just "input", "output", and "output"). These three steps must be followed in order to successfully compile a Java program. This means that in order for the program to work, you must perform the following steps:

The first step is to enter a value. This means that the program requires information from the user, which is typically provided by telling the computer what you want to be done and how you want it done. If you have a variable called "x," you would enter it as follows: int x = 1.

As a result, the computer understands that this should be interpreted as an integer (i.e., a whole number) value (1). Inputs are the values that we enter into data-driven programs.

-2. The transformation step comes next. This means that the program must use the variable in some way. This is a much more complicated step, but what it really means is that we need to show our users how things are changing in response to their input (or, in other words, offering them information). If you had a variable called "myAge" and you wanted to write your name based on its value, you could do so as follows:

system.out.println ("Hello myAge")

This would cause the program's output to change whenever myAge changed (i.e. every time the user changed their age). Outputs are the values that we enter into programs.

The third and final step is output. This means that the program must save or print the data it has worked with so that it can be saved elsewhere (usually on a hard drive, memory stick, etc.). This is a simple step because all you have to do is use something like this:

system.out.println ("Hello myAge")

You could do something like this to save what was done in our program (for example, print out "hello myAge") to a separate file:

system.out.println ("Hello myAge").

CHAPTER 14:

OBJECT-ORIENTED PROGRAMMING?

Object-Oriented Programming (OOP) is a programming paradigm that makes use of objects and how they interact with one another. In contrast to pure procedural programming, objects are data structures that contain both data and functions that operate on them.

What Exactly Is Object-Oriented Programming?

Object-oriented programming is a technique for simplifying development by breaking down complex algorithms into simpler, more manageable parts. The complexity of OOP is derived from the relationship between these objects and how they interact with one another, rather than from how they process information internally.

What Doesn't Object-Oriented Programming Entail?

In contrast to OOP, is a frequently misunderstood programming approach that advocates programming every object as if it were a real object when it isn't. OOP refers to the programming style used in object-oriented applications. It does not refer to the language or methodology; each language and design technique can be used independently of the others; rather, it refers to how objects are treated.

An object-oriented program can be written in any language that supports data abstraction and inheritance concepts. However, in addition to these fundamental goals, OOP offers several advantages over traditional approaches to software development.

Object-Oriented Programming: What Are the Benefits?

OOP has a number of distinct advantages, which include:

1. OOP Promotes Modular Development. The whole point of OOP is to break programs down into smaller, more manageable pieces. This allows each component to be implemented in a short period of time and then easily maintained. Rather than having objects inherit from a base class, the relationship between these parts is designed so that each object is easily identifiable with a single function - e.g. Class.new() called on the class name - which is invoked by passing in one or more parameters - e.g. "objectId."

<functionName>().

2. Object-oriented interfaces expose unnecessary complications. In an object-oriented system based on inheritance and polymorphic behavior, OOP has the advantage of displaying unnecessary complexity. When a programmer creates a new object in C++, for example, he or she must either define all of the internal functions or leave them undefined. If he leaves them undefined,

69

they will almost certainly cause bugs in the program; however, if he defines them all, he is duplicating functionality, as there is no way for that newly created object to communicate appropriately with other objects.

3. Data transparency aids in the avoidance of bugs. Transparency of data also aids in the avoidance of bugs. In an object-oriented program, for example, if a programmer wants to check whether a variable is less than five, it is easier to say if (x 5) than if (x = 5). This is due to the fact that the first expression clearly demonstrates the programmer's intention. The second expression necessitates the reader inferring what it truly means.

4. OOP Promotes Code Reuse Object-oriented programming allows objects to be combined and inherited from other objects, which increases code reuse. The programmer must write the program twice in procedural programming, once for each case. Furthermore, with OOP, the programmer can use a library of previously written code and only need to rewrite a small section to interface with his own code.

5. OOP is simple to maintain. Any change to the code in procedural programming necessitates changes to all functions that call that code. If a function or method is changed or added in OOP, only that function or procedure must be altered.

6. OOP is simple to learn and use due to its modularity and simple modular decomposition. The programmer is encouraged to think of objects, their relationships, and functions as modular sets of reusable parts when using OOP.

7. OOP Promotes Good Code Design. By providing structures that encourage good programming practice, OOP encourages good coding practice. In C++, for example, there are separate (sealed) classes for representing data and performing operations on that

data, and in Java, there is a corresponding package for the same purpose.

8. Modularity reduces the possibility of errors caused by a single mistake.

Because OOP allows for modularization, if an error occurs in one module, it will not affect other modules because each module has a unique interface to other modules, allowing each module to function independently of the others.

9. OOP is less difficult to debug and maintain. This is due to the programmer's code having fewer functions, which can lead to bugs. Furthermore, because each class has a unique interface to other classes, there is less chance that two classes will be connected incorrectly.

10. Objects can be manipulated and designed in a modular fashion more easily than procedural objects of the same type. An object in OOP is more easily manipulated and designed in a modular manner than procedural objects of the same type - for example, object creation or destruction.

11. Data encapsulation facilitates variable assignment and, as a result, reduces the possibility of errors caused by insufficient input.

12. Function encapsulation to data makes reuse more feasible, reducing the possibility of errors caused by re-inventing the wheel.

13. Object-oriented languages are simpler to learn and thus provide a more intuitive user interface than other languages. The simplicity of OOP is demonstrated by teaching methodologies such as object-oriented programming courses in universities.

14. Code encapsulation makes it easier to integrate a component into an existing system. If the function is encapsulated

in one or more objects, changes to that function are isolated from the rest of the program's functions. Furthermore, if the function is encapsulated in one or more objects, it can be inserted into another program by simply copying the object into the appropriate location.

15. Data encapsulation promotes program modularity, allowing programmers to create programs that are easily adaptable to change.

16. The expressive capability of object-oriented programming languages provides programmers with a precise and economical way of expressing their intentions in small amounts of code.

17. Data encapsulation encourages data hiding, which helps to eliminate many security issues.

18. Encapsulation encourages programmers to think of code as self-contained modules that are easier to debug and maintain than code that is susceptible to external interference.

19. Encapsulation reduces a program's complexity. Because there is less chance that another part of the program will affect the function being changed, it makes it easier for the programmer to find and fix bugs (because the function is encapsulated into an object).

CHAPTER 15:

CLIENT-SERVER APPLICATIONS?

In a nutshell, client-server applications are computer programs that include both a local and a remote component. The client (such as your web browser) is the local component, and the server (the software you're using) is the remote component. Data is passed from one to the other. When attempting to access an online application, a user enters their username and password on their local machine, requesting access from a remote server. The beauty of these apps is that there is a thin line between what your computer can do and what happens on a remote machine. This means that even if you only have a basic understanding of coding, you can create games or other high-quality software.

The root vegetable turnip

A turnip, for example, is a small object that can represent a username, password, or any other type of encryption on the client. We can make our lives much easier by using this simple coding trick:

In this case: A turnip Turnip B=B turnip Brussels C=C D=D turnips become E=E turnips. F=F lettuce transforms into G=G lettuce. We don't need to use encryption every time we communicate with the server; instead, we can use this trick.

Coding Fundamentals

Languages implement features in a variety of ways. C is one of those languages that have more capabilities than Java or Python. Ignoring these differences is not permitted because it will prevent the code from running correctly. To begin, we must learn about all of these distinctions and how they should be applied.

In general, there are four types of statements: if statements, for loops, while loops, and switch blocks.

The If Clause

Before executing a specific block of action, you can use this statement to determine whether a specific condition is true or false. This statement is used several times in our turnip example code above to determine whether 1 turnip sprouts 2 sprouts. 3 becomes 4 lettuce or any other number between 0 and 5.

When a statement completes, the variable is moved up one position by default, but you can move it manually in the if statement.

Allow us to go through integers or any other list of objects in loops. They come in handy when writing simple, repetitive code. For example, if we wanted to print out all of our turnip's turns, we could write it as follows:

In our turnip example, we'll have lettuce seeds, sprouts (1 - 3), lettuce (4 - 5), sprouts (6 - 9), and so on. Every time we run the loop, we will print the number between the square brackets.

Before checking and executing a block of code, the while loop determines whether a specific condition is true or false. The code inside the curly brackets is executed at least once, but it is terminated when a specific condition is met. This while loop could be used to randomly select one item from our basket. The code enclosed by curly brackets will be run at least once. It will not run again, however, until we assign something to turnip Sprouts in line 5.

The statement of change

This statement allows you to determine whether a condition is true or false and then jump to a specific block of code based on the result. In our turnip-sprouting example, we could simulate this by using different numbers to represent the number of sprouts, beginning with 1:

When we say that "statements inside the curly brackets are executed at least once," we mean exactly once. However, if we don't assign anything to turnip Sprouts, all of these statements will be executed only once! By placing case statements above each section of code, we can instruct the switch statement. We can write the following case statements in our example:

Case 1: A=1, B=2, C=4, D=1, E=2, F=3, G=5. In case 2, A = 2, B = 3, C = 4, and D = 5.

Case Statement Alternatives

When it comes to writing case statements, you have a few options. You can specify whether or not the statement should be executed. You can examine the statement to see if there is an exception on either side. If no case statement matches it, you can also add a default statement. Here's what our code would look like if we used the proper syntax: In this case, it will not only check A to see if it is one, two, three, or four...but it will also check B to see if C is between one and five. If neither of those conditions is met, the default statement at the end will be executed. The idea behind using these three statements in a row is that the while statement determines which code block is executed and when the for loop returns a new value for an iteration.

A C program's general structure is to include the header files, declare the variables and functions that you intend to use, and then write the code.

Two header files will be used in this program. One will govern how we handle input and output (stdio.h), and the other will enable us to generate random numbers (random.h). We'll declare our variables at the top of main(), where they'll be accessible throughout the program. Lines 8-12 use the while statement to read user input until enter is pressed, and it stores each value in turnip after separating them with commas. In lines 16-22, a for loop prints out the number of times each turnip has sprouted, and we finish the program with a semicolon.

stdio.h> should be included. #include 'random.h' main() is an int function. Reads user input and stores it in turnip int A, B, C; while(inkey())

/ Save input into turnipA variable, then loop until invalidated A = readkey(); / Get next keystroke if (A == "1") / If the user typed in 1, print the maximum number of sprouts (n) for each turnip. "You have n sprouts for a total of n." printf("You have n sprouts for a total of n."); if (A == "2") / If the user typed in 2, print the average number of sprouts (avg) for each turnip.

CHAPTER 16:

LOGGING IN TO PROGRAMS

Programs are the fundamental building blocks of coding. Without a computer, programs can be run by writing them down on paper, typing them into an online editor, or talking through their steps aloud. Most programs are divided into two sections: (1) telling the computer what to do and (2) instructing the computer on how to do it. The first part is known as the command, and it instructs the computer on what operations to perform, such as adding two numbers or erasing a file. The second part is known as the instruction method, and it describes how to perform these operations, such as addition or using the erase function in a word processing program.

To begin, learn a simple program that will teach you the difference between commands and instructions.

"Hello, World!" is the command (i.e., "Write your name on the screen."

Instructions: (1) write your name from what line of your program, (2) is it centered or justified, and (3) does it have any special formatting?

Commands consist of a single word. They instruct the computer on what to do. "Write your name on the screen," for example, could be one command. You don't want to be concerned about how computer memory space is organized or how to format things for display output! The computer simply performs them for you. In fact, the computer does all of the work.

Instructions, on the other hand, tell the computer what to do. "Write your name on the screen," for example. This instructs the computer on how to display your name on the screen. Some instructions necessitate a little more detail. As an example:

(1) Where do you write your name in your program, (2) is it centered or justified, and (3) does it have any special formatting?

Instructions not only tell you what to do but also how to do it! As a result, they are referred to as "instructions." As an example: "Fill in your name on the screen. The center is justified." This instructs the computer to write your name in the center of the page.

There are various types of instructions. If you want to include a number, write something like this:

number = 1 + number Alternatively, you could express the instruction directly as follows:

number = 1 + number Fill in your name in the center, center justified. Increase the number line by one.

It irritates me when you don't write the entire step-by-step procedure in a single command or instruction in a program. Instead, each piece of information is usually divided into several smaller instructions known as statements. In the preceding examples, for example, there are two distinct instructions: (1) Formalized paraphrase ""Write your name here," and (2) "Center justified." Fill in your name." However, they are really one statement that you have broken down into smaller pieces.

Statements or lines of code can be used to represent "commands" and "instruction methods" in code or computer programs. A program is made up of separate instructions and commands that are written line by line. This is how programs work; each line does a single task.

When writing your programs on paper or in an online editor like Notepad++, divide your instructions into multiple steps so that each line contains only one instruction. It is critical to keep each instruction on a separate line of code to demonstrate what the computer is doing. For example, if your program contains the instruction "Add one to the number line," it is too long to fit on a single line. It would be preferable if you wrote something like this:

number = 1 + number

Or, if your program instructs you to "Write your name," this is too short to fit on a single line. It would be preferable if you wrote something like this:

What to do, write your name.

It is clear what the computer is doing when each statement is on its own line of code. When we begin writing programs in Python and Ruby, you will learn which commands tell the computer what to do and which lines specify how it does it.

CHAPTER 17:

LOGICAL PROGRAM GROUPING - BASIC SYNTAX

-Program Declarations

-Labels and line numbers

-Optimizing Coding to Achieve the Best Practice

-Procedures and Functions

-Strings and arrays (and Their Relationship to One Another)

-Programs with Conditional Execution

Debugging Programs Without a Debugger - Examining the machine code of compiled programs at run time with GDB and GNU Debugger (GDB) (command-line source code debugger). Set a breakpoint and run your program after compiling it with debug information. GDB will put the program to a halt at the breakpoint. This guides you through the process of inspecting all of your program's machine-level details (its source code, including debug information) and allowing you to deal with 'live' problems.

Coding Requirements

Coding style is influenced by how you think about memory, variables, and file I/O. If your coding style is similar to that of others, it will make your life easier. However, the coding style may cause annoyance if it differs from that of others. Essentially, there are two approaches to this: obsess over minute details or err on the side of caution when making changes. Most of us fall somewhere in the middle, and it all depends on what works best for you.

I prefer to use as few curly braces as possible and to avoid the use of parenthesis whenever possible. Most people, on the other hand, use every curly brace they can get their hands on and add new parentheses wherever they think they are needed. Almost always, there is a way to get what you want without using unnecessary parenthesis. Second, never 'parenthesize yourself into the ground' with extra brackets and braces unless you (or someone else) have told you that this is required for their specific program or library. (It's your life, your decision, but keep in mind that they're there for a reason.)

Examples of Coding Styles

The following example is provided by the author of this book. It's not perfect, but it's close. Excellent examples can be found in the Wikipedia book on C/AL (Clike syntax). I've included a link to it further down the page. The following topics are covered:

"HOTSPOT PLACEMENT" (code hot spot placement) "VARIABLE NAMES" (variable naming in general), which is a relatively brief description (one paragraph). It's a small area that deserves only a passing mention.

"MEMORY MANAGEMENT" (code memory management which is seriously flawed)

"EXAMPLE OF A PROBLEM" (code problem example). "Programs that no longer exist"

"(a) Using the pointer a, execute a statement. Keep a record of what you've done with a variable called name. Use the address of that variable to keep track of where you are right now."

"A - Repeat this with the pointer a. The program will print a message for each step that it takes. The offset to the next line should be stored in the location."

"B - Write some code to accomplish this. Print the name of each line in the loop (from 1 to n) using a pointer variable called name."

"(b) - Add another method and print out your results so far."

"C - Add another loop and use handmade to hide your window from view rather than hiding it entirely from clicks. HIDE or SHOW the window if it is 'hidden' by this hot spot." "

84

"D - Insert some code to create a hotspot for yourself. Create a hot spot for each of the following lines: 1 to n, 1 to n-1, and 1 to n+1."

"E - Restart your program. "(a) - Create a function, then go back in time and do it all over again." (b) Make a call to it from the main program." "CODE \sEXAMPLE" See "Source Code B-01" on page 48 of this source file for more information (here). In addition, see "Source Code B-02" on page 49 of this source file (here).

"Programmers who use this coding style tend to write code that is elegant and clean. Their code is similar to that of a good high school math homework problem."

CHAPTER 18:

DEPLOYING PROGRAMS

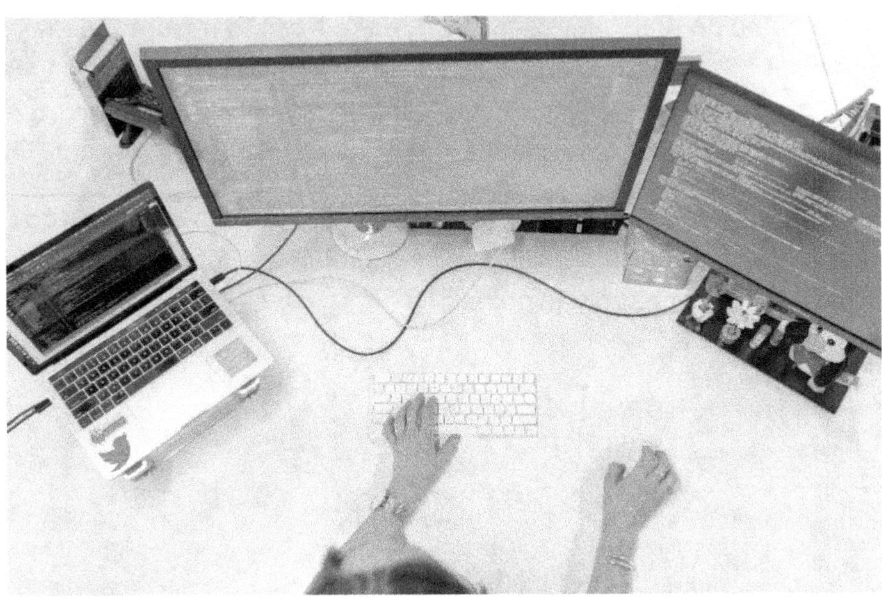

The internet has transformed how we work, interact, and live. Online tools are used to easily create, store, and share information. Nowadays, you can code in your own language on almost any device - learn how to deploy programs online before it's too late!

These platforms have been developed to save time as a result of technological advancements over the last decade or so. For coding jobs, you no longer need a degree in computer programming; you can become an online programmer with little-to-no experience if you want! Some of these platforms are free, while others require payment. For beginners, it is recommended that you begin with free platforms so that you can determine whether you want to become a full-time programmer.

The most significant advantage of using online coding platforms is that they are accessible from any device. They are also available 24 hours a day, seven days a week, which means you can work at any time of day or night if you have an internet connection and know how to code. However, this could be a disadvantage for those looking for part-time work, as most of these platforms require users to be constantly online in order to function properly.

The disadvantages of these platforms are that they are extremely restrictive in terms of what can be coded in each platform. While you can use your own code, there will be some areas that you will be unable to access. For example, they may not permit you to develop your own games or applications. In general, before asking for money, these platforms necessitate a significant amount of time and dedication.

There are numerous online coding platforms available today, each with its own set of advantages and disadvantages. Let's take a look at some of 2018's most popular platforms:

W3Schools

It is currently one of the most popular coding platforms. It has tutorials for both beginners and experts. English, Spanish, French, German, and Russian are among the languages supported by the tutorials. It contains tutorials for all types of coding, such as web design, web development, and front-end development. W3Schools also provides easy-to-understand documentation on code and other computer programming topics.

Codecademy

Codecademy is another excellent platform for beginners to learn how to code. This one includes courses in over a dozen languages, including JavaScript, Ruby, HTML/CSS, and PHP. It is best suited for those interested in web design or development. It also has a mobile app, allowing you to use it from anywhere. The interface is simple to understand and use, which is one of the tutorial's main advantages.

The Khan Academy

It offers classes in over 20 subjects, including math, science, computer science, history, and many others. HTML, CSS, and JavaScript are just a few of the tutorials available. It is a free learning platform that provides its users with excellent tutorials and support. When it comes to coding, it is not as simple to use, but it is still an excellent learning platform.

The Code Academy

Code Academy has created some of the most effective digital programming learning tools available today. The website contains over 1000 programming instructional videos for both experts and beginners. If you know what you're doing, many of these programs can be used to launch a career in computer programming. Many schools have also used it to teach students the fundamentals of coding and website creation. Python, PHP, HTML/CSS, JavaScript, Ruby, and Java are among the languages it teaches.

Udemy

Udemy is a fantastic online learning platform for learning how to code. It has thousands of paid courses that anyone who wants to learn more about the technical aspects of coding can take for free. Some of these courses are free, while others require payment. It is one of the most popular online platforms for learning computer programming. The website also showcases projects created by users all over the world using various coding languages and platforms. It also provides certification in some areas, such as Android development. There are numerous other platforms available today from which to learn. It all boils down to what you want from a learning system. If you decide it's time to start pursuing an online career, don't forget to look into these coding platforms first. They can assist you in the pursuit of your goals.

CHAPTER 19:

INTERNET PROGRAMMING

Internet programming is a skill that allows you to create or change the dynamics of any website. How do you know if coding for the table is a good idea? If your answer is "I'm not sure," this book is for you! We'll be able to promote more efficient ways to achieve our goals if we understand how programming and computer science work. We'll apply programming fundamentals to an example problem using code written by beginners in the past.

Making changes to a website is one of the most valuable skills for a website owner. Consider what you do on your website. Many websites, such as blogs and forums, provide opportunities for self-expression and interaction with other users. There are also numerous options for site navigation, search, and discovery. People will schedule games on other sites, such as sports forums and news sites, to find opponents or books to read. Some websites require functionality that can only be provided by a programmer. If you want your site to get more visitors or become more popular, you'll need the programming power available from Table coder (tablecoder.com).

Programming is a broad term that refers to the creation of programs that are simple to understand and execute. Coding gives website owners the ability to modify or change a site after it has been created. Many sites created by non-programmers in the past have made it simple to change content and functionality without understanding how code works or what makes a particular code more efficient. Other times, you must spend time learning how things work through trial and error before you can make your site more valuable.

Programming is one of those specialized fields that takes years to master. To learn the necessary skills for success, patience, dedication, and self-education are required. The desire to learn as much as possible is one of the most important skills you can have.

91

When you know enough to write your programs, it will be easier to donate or sell new features.

It's impossible... There's no way!

So many websites are available in the world today. It's difficult to keep up with them all. How are you supposed to keep up with all of the new games, events, and groups? How will you ever find something interesting enough to learn more about? The answer is straightforward: YOU CAN! You have the opportunity to work as a coder for your website. As a coder, you will be able to write functions that alter the behavior of your website. Adding plugins that add functionality without knowing how it works will be one of the most significant changes you'll make.

Experience gained in other areas helps to establish the skills required to become a good coder. Coding is more than just writing code with special characters (though that isn't necessarily a bad thing).

What exactly is programming?

Programming is the process of using a computer to solve problems. There are many aspects to programming, but none is more important than understanding how a computer works and how code can be used to control it. When discussing how to use code for your site, this section will concentrate on the fundamentals.

The image below depicts a fictitious computer screen. "Stack Overflow" is the title at the top. It is a website where programmers can ask questions and solve problems (and give answers, too). The program in this example has many features that assist guests in locating solutions to programming problems.

Tag clouds are a feature on the right side of the computer screen. This is a graphical representation of the most commonly used tags concerning a problem. It's similar to an index of well-known words and phrases used on the site when writing code.

If you want to learn more about programming, go to the Stack Overflow site and learn more about Stack Overflow.

Problem Solving in Programming

We'll assume you have no prior experience with computer science or programming. You'll probably be interested in using the Table coder (http://tablecoder.com) to add features to your site rather than learning how to code a program from scratch. Solving problems is an excellent way to get started with programming. It's a powerful tool that can be used to accomplish a variety of tasks. A problem is something that needs to be fixed or should be fixed.

Before you can solve a problem, you must first identify it. "Defining the terms" is a term used by programmers to describe how they understand something. That is, before you can do anything with words, you must first understand what they mean (especially before you can program them).

A computer language defines terms for problem-solving and programming by using special characters. Code is a set of instructions that tells a computer what to do. Variables are special characters and symbols that allow you to read, write, and change code.

The image below depicts a desk with papers and pens strewn about it. The papers and pens have been sorted by color, size, and shape. If you want to try it at home, follow these steps:

Begin by gathering all of the blue pens on your desk (they're most likely under your laptop).

93

Return them to the "blue" box. Please pick up all of the green pens and return them to their proper places.

We'll refer to this as the "green" box.

After you've collected all of the pens, carefully place them back in their box. It will be clear that all of the pens have been organized. Each pen has a designated location, and there is a method for determining which pen belongs where.

We can organize anything in our homes or businesses using this method.

We could choose to organize anything from food to furniture or even work-related documents (like your paycheck). We could also use this system to organize computer files, such as those containing photos of your family and important documents from your tax return.

CHAPTER 20:

PROGRAMMING FOR MOBILE DEVICES

Coding is a skill with enormous value and interest, but it can appear to be a daunting task. In this post, we'll go over the fundamentals of HTML5 coding for mobile devices. It's intimidating at first, but once you learn the language, you'll have access to a world of opportunities...

The Fundamentals: The Code Language

Coding is frequently thought to be a specialized jargon used only by expert programmers. In reality, they're just speaking in their language!

Programming languages are simply languages that people use to describe how software should work. People use natural languages when they speak English, French, or Spanish. Programming languages are artificial languages designed to communicate with software. In this post, we'll look at how to code for mobile devices with HTML5.

HTML5 is a markup language that is used to create web pages. HTML5 may already be used in your Facebook posts and Twitter messages. This language is used to create websites that can be accessed via the internet by all computers (not just mobile devices). You won't have to worry about your HTML5 code not working on someone else's device because it's a standard.

What Exactly Is HTML?

HTML is an abbreviation for Hypertext Markup Language. It's also referred to as a web markup language or just plain old markup language (PLA). It was invented in the 1990s and can still be found in many online magazines and newspapers today. This language is probably familiar to you because it is used to create all of those fancy websites that we see every day! You may have even created your own basic websites in HTML in the past...but the basics are just that. Let's get to the meat of the matter!

HTML5 includes a number of new features that allow you to create more interactive websites. We'll only be using a few of these, but feel free to experiment with the others on your own. CSS3, which we'll learn about in another post, is another exciting option!

!DOCTYPE HTML> Let's Get Started

The first thing you should learn is how to create a basic HTML5 document. Don't be alarmed! To begin, it's simpler than you might think. HTML5 is much easier to use than HTML4, which makes use of more complex tags and syntax. HTML5 employs self-explanatory semantic tags.

The first line of code you need to write to create a new HTML document is:

!DOCTYPE html>>>>>>>>>>>>>>>>>>>>

HTML5 includes a number of different doctypes (instructions for how the documents are being created). The above doctype is the most widely used for creating web pages. This code consists of only two letters (html) in all lowercase, with no suffixes or prefixes. To the rest of the world, it simply stands for "HTML."

It almost looks like English when written like this. This is because HTML5 preserves what is known as a case in other languages: upper case letters, capital letters in between two lower case letters, and so on. There are, however, some exceptions:

- In HTML, all cross-references (links) use instead of '. Capitalization is used for proper nouns (i.e. Nyan Cat). - The entire character set of punctuation marks has been chosen (a handful like the full stop or the question mark). - Instead of italics, *asterisks* are used to indicate emphasis. - Hyphens are used to separate spaces (for example, 11.*1234*).

Even if you don't use this exact syntax, you can still create websites using many of the syntax rules it specifies. The most important is that every nook and cranny of a webpage should have a tag identifying what it is. We use language to communicate on the internet in the same way that we would speak to each other in English.

Let's get started with HTML5! The Section HEAD>

HTML5 employs a head> section, which processes data before the actual document is displayed on a screen. Consider the head> section to be a preface in which you list all of your text's important information. HTML5 Fundamentals Let's begin with our first HTML document! The HEAD> section would look like this:

!DOCTYPE html>!DOCTYPE html lang=en> <head> The title of your website should be listed here in both English and the programming language you've chosen. /html> /head>

The general rule for title> tags is that they should be capitalized, followed by a space, and then the name. This should then be placed at the top of your page (between the html>/head> tags). When creating a mobile website, keep in mind that only the first title> tag should be used. This will give your page its own unique ID, known as a Web Title. Because HTML5 has a new way of doing this with a meta tag called "data-web-title=", it's critical that you keep track of this value for future references (as you will for all of the other tags you'll be using).

The only other thing worth mentioning is how your website's title works. The concept of "page" in HTML4 was very different from what we know today. It referred to what we now call "web pages." The title was more of a "title tag" in that case, and it was independent of the document you were reading.

The Web Title and Page Title in HTML5 are distinct!

To begin, a Web Title is used to generate a unique identification value for each page of your website. This is required to avoid multiple pages with the same name (like what might happen if you made a mistake while writing your webpage). As a result, each web page has its own unique ID (referred to as a web title), which is listed in the title> tag. The title> tag will appear above the opening html>/head> tag and prior to any other content.

CHAPTER 21.

DISTINCTION JAVA, PYTHON, AND C++ ARE THE THREE MOST POPULAR PROGRAMMING LANGUAGES.

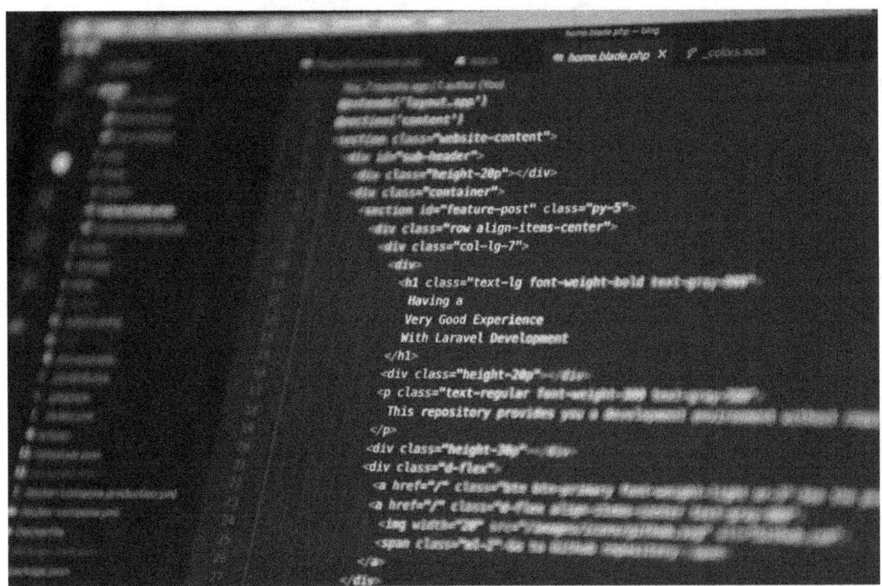

Python is an object-oriented programming language that is frequently used for web development and scripting. It differs from other high-level languages such as Java and C++ in that it combines procedural and dynamic typing with syntax that is similar to English words. Java, on the other hand, is a statically typed object-oriented language geared toward distributed computing systems that web developers can use to create server-side applications or system software.

Unlike Python's English-like syntax, C++ has its own set of rules for declaring variables with keywords like "int," "float," and "char."

So, what are the differences between these three programming languages? A simple answer would be that Python focuses on the code, whereas Java and C++ focus on the compiler. Let's take a quick look at this statement in terms of each programming language.

In Python, the code is regarded as primary and is given precedence over the compiler. In contrast to Java, where all classes must be named after a class name and its respective package name, e.g. java.util.ArrayList, Python has no strict rules for naming conventions. In Python, all that matters is that a class or function exists.

Rather than the syntax, Python recognizes the existence of objects and executes them. In addition, there are no strict rules for indentation in Python, so indentations have no effect on code execution. A programmer can write code with multiple nested loops and function levels without worrying about the number of spaces between them.

In Java, on the other hand, compiler rules are considered more important than the code itself, resulting in a limited number of things a programmer can do when compared to Python or C++ programmers. Java, in particular, emphasizes object-oriented programming over procedural programming, as demonstrated by C++'s templates and macros features. The manner in which a programmer writes code is given greater weight than the manner in which the code can be executed, which confuses Java developers who are used to coding in Python.

Finally, Python focuses on the code, Java on the compiler rules, and C++ on both. In terms of language design, an experienced programmer would be better off learning C++ because he or she will be able to understand how a compiler works at a low level, whereas learning object-oriented programming in Java will be difficult. Python would be preferable to Java and C++ for an inexperienced programmer looking for a more approachable programming language to learn due to its shorter syntax lengths.

CONCLUSION

Coding is the process of manipulating data with a computer program (or software) for use in various applications. It is a type of programming. Programming languages are used to code and program, allowing for more complex tasks to be completed than would be possible by handwriting code. Coding is an essential part of many people's daily lives around the world, from business professionals and engineers to designers and those who teach students how to code in school.

Schools across the country are teaching coding to students for a variety of reasons. It is not only an important part of modern life, but it also allows people to complete tasks more efficiently. It also makes later years of learning how to program computers easier, allowing for skills relevant to future professions. Coding is also an excellent way to foster students' creativity and problem-solving abilities, which will be useful in a variety of future endeavors.

So, what is it about coding that can pique students' interest? What about the process that can pique their interest and entice them to learn more? Fortunately, it's not that difficult.

Based on my own experiences, here are some ideas to get you started on your coding journey:

Programming passion – This may appear to be a no-brainer at first, but it is true. For many people, programming is not only a means of achieving a specific goal (such as earning money), but it is also a source of personal fulfillment. Coding is not only enjoyable for many people, but it also makes them happy in the long run. Coding allows students to truly express themselves creatively, both in their code and in the manner in which they create it. Over time, programming can be very therapeutic for people.

Real-life application – Many people do not pursue a career in programming because it is enjoyable. They do so because they believe it will have a practical application in the future. This is true of almost any academic subject, and it is unquestionably true of coding. In fact, many people choose to study a specific course of action solely because they believe their skills will be useful in the job market or will help them achieve their ideal future career situation. In fact, many students intend to pursue a career as a programmer after graduation.

Making something interesting and practical – It is much easier to learn something that will be useful in the long run than a less useful subject with no reason to learn. Coding is said to provide long-term benefits for those who enjoy it and will aid in the development of future professional skills.

Coding enables people to create something they are proud of. Many students will find this extremely motivating. Because there are no set rules or boundaries in programming, students can be as creative as they want, resulting in something exciting and valuable. This is extremely motivating and exciting for students; after all, that is why they want to learn coding in the first place – they enjoy making things!